Walter J. Reum

Gerald C. Mattran

10/23/66

Politics from the inside up

⊠ Politics
from the inside up

WALTER J. REUM
and
GERALD C. MATTRAN

 FOLLETT PUBLISHING COMPANY
Chicago / New York 1966

*Drawings by Francis Sho Kaihatsu and
Claude Zajakowski*

Copyright © 1966 by Walter J. Reum and Gerald C. Mattran

Library of Congress Catalog Card Number: 66-28918

First Printing

Manufactured in the United States of America

Follett Publishing Company
1010 West Washington Boulevard
Chicago, Illinois 60607

T7225

To *Lucy Reum* and *Nancy Mattran*

⊠ **Contents**

⊠ Introduction

This is a book about politics and politicians. It is not a repetition of often-stated value judgments. A politician is "good" to the extent that he performs the necessary functions of government properly; he is "bad" to the extent that he uses the powers of public office for personal gain. But since we cannot adequately define "properly" and "personal gain," we cannot determine degrees of goodness or badness. Nor will we try. But we can and do try to show the *how* of the politician; how he gets started, how he progresses, and how he achieves success.

Politics from the Inside Up is a book that shows the inside of politics as it operates practically, not idealistically. It presents, not the headlines, but the goings-on that never make the news at all. By so doing, the book becomes an explanation of the politician, rather than an apology for or an indictment of him.

To explain the politician, one must first know who he is. The category is broad, so a definition is easy: A politician is anyone involved in the intricacies of seeking or holding elective office. United States Senators are politicians, and so are precinct captains. Governors, congressmen, auditors, clerks—all are politicians. So are envelope-sealers, doorbell pounders, handbill distributors, and campaign contributors. There are, of course, apparent differences among those who come within the overall definition. But the bonds of identity are shared and sharable because the prime motivation is the same for all politicians.

Make no mistake about it: every politician aspires, either to office or to higher office. Thus the prime motivation is the need to be elected. A politician out of office is a nullity. In office, he has attained his desires: he has power and position; he is successful. The need for office makes the American politician unique, both in and out of his environment. The politician is different from other Americans and from the politician in other countries. He is compelled to live in a milieu, created by our system of government, that has no place for a loser.

Not only did the framers of the Constitution ignore the loser, they ignored the politician altogether. At least, parties (the cradles of all politicians) were not mentioned. There is even evidence, as in Number 10 of *The Federalist* written by Madison, that the framers felt that parties could not arise in a system such as they had created. They were wrong. Parties have developed, and they have developed to the point where they tend to control the system.

Nor did it take long for the party spirit to begin to grow. In Washington's administration difficulties quickly developed between Jefferson and Hamilton. Their differences in opinion and philosophy were basic, and their high positions in the cabinet made the differences more acute. Each had an attentive group of followers, and from these followers came the disciples who form the nucleus of parties.

When Jefferson became President, he developed some of the basic formulas of executive control over the legislature, thus creating a locus of party leadership. From that time to this, the President has been the leader of his political party.

Later, Andrew Jackson developed and formalized the patronage system by which loyal party members are rewarded for their faith. Jackson depended on workers at the lowest levels to win his presidential victories, and to retain their loyalty, he rewarded them. The system remains in use today.

By Lincoln's day, parties were well enough developed for him to compose a set of rules for effective local canvassing. A master politician, he waited until the new Republican party had built a local organization in Illinois before he would become a member of it. Some say he never was a Republican, but always remained a Whig, using the new party only as a vehicle for his own ambitions.

The development of parties and party systems under the Constitution has not been without its saving aspects. Had it not been for the development of parties, the Constitution itself might not have the flexibility that has given it longevity. This can be seen by comparison of the federal government's present position on civil rights with the positions held in 1856, 1866, and 1900. In each instance, the majority party supported those ideas that, at the very least, would not keep it from being elected.

Within our governmental system, then, all politicians are forced to operate under the aegis of party. Which party makes relatively little difference, for the parties are basically the same. The success of the party is the success of each individual in it and is the end for which all work. Success is not only a goal to be sought now, for its present fruit; success now is a requirement for success in the future, since in politics victory tends to propagate victory.

The party in power has jobs with which to reward the faithful, and the offices it holds may be used for dispensing favors to court the electorate. Favors are important. People will become more excited by a hole in the street in front of their house or by a traffic ticket than they will by the question of admitting Red China to the U.N. Are the people wrong? To some degree yes. They are wrong when they try to hide from conflict, as when they complain because "Batman" is interrupted by a television report on a serious crisis in space. But there is yet another problem—the sheer size of government and the quantity of decisions to be made.

Even as we are writing this, village, township, county, state, and, of course, federal governments are acting on matters of interest to us. As politicians, we are intimately concerned. But there are simply too many issues for us to absorb them all. For those whose interest in government is less than intense, the burden becomes overwhelming. Thus the individual citizen's reaction is to back away from every issue that is not well publicized, and thus not easily comprehended and decided. The electorate responds to the complexity of government by withdrawal rather than by increased interest and effort.

Politicians realize all this. So the parties develop precinct workers who function as semiofficial ombudsmen, who see to it that all the voters receive everything they have coming from government. Naturally, a worker can perform this task much better when his party is in power.

Such is the world in which our hero, Franklin Pierce Small, chooses to live. It is a politician's world, more specifically, a world of party politicians. It is a world both metropolitan and middle class. Small lives in a city, and he is neither poor nor wealthy. He is average in most respects, except in the possession of one quality, which he has in abundance: desire. He wants political success, and he wants it badly enough to make those personal and family sacrifices required for success. This desire, combined with a learned shrewdness and an ability to observe, makes him a successful politician. Like others, Small must learn the ways of the politician if he is to succeed. There is no natural politician.

Among the many lessons to be learned are the need to defer, abjectly at first, to party leaders; and the need to become totally involved. Ways to excite people must be learned, and how a proper image can be developed. Once learned, these lessons are never forgotten. This, unfortunately, is the most regrettable aspect of the politician's story. The qualities he learns to value are those least needed in an effective government official. Political success can never be equated with governmental success.

The need to be elected and re-elected, the power of parties, and the nature of the system combine to create a caste of politicians, and they, alas, are governed only by expediency.

WALTER J. REUM & GERALD C. MATTRAN
Oak Park, Illinois
September, 1966

⊠ Disclaimer

The authors assume no responsibility for the results of following the rules outlined here. Nor do they assume responsibility for the effects on the governments of the several states when all elective offices are held by those who have followed the rules.

⊠ **Prologue**

So you want to be Governor? Then take off your personality before you start reading. There are rules to follow, and they must be followed exactly. You must be psychologically nude at the start to be properly fitted with the correct mental and emotional uniform.

If at any point you find the price of becoming Governor too high...quit. But pass the book along to a friend who *will* pay the price. Then become the power behind *him*. In many ways, that's better than being Governor anyway.

⊠ **Before politics**

You, Franklin Pierce Small, have just been defeated for the office of Guardian of the Keys to the Lower Staircase of your local Wallaby Lodge. Bitterly, you listen as the Secretary pronounces the results:

ALLEN JACKSON	123,
FRANKLIN PIERCE SMALL	13.

After all, you're young, smart, active, ready-and-willing. You spent a year working toward this chance to run for office in the lodge, and now look what's happened . . . Just look!

But don't give up. There is still a way for you to find the happiness you want. POLITICS!

You're interested in politics, or you wouldn't be reading this book. And you want to be Governor.

At least. If you follow the rules you *can* become Governor of your state—easier than you can become Most High Dingo of the Wallabys. And you can do it quicker.

In politics, there are ways to overcome the difficulties you encountered in the Wallabys. You'll still find older members who think you should sit quietly for the first fifteen years or so while learning maturity from them over the bar. But their attitude, as you will see, can be turned into a plus for you. Just bear this in mind when the going gets rough: You, Franklin Pierce Small, CAN be Governor . . . at least!

By the way, if your name is not Franklin Pierce Small,

RULE 1. *Change your name.*

Stan Wojakowski has limited public appeal. Yours is a perfect name, Franklin Pierce Small. (People won't remember where they heard it, but they'll know they heard it some place.) A good political name should be deceptively similar to one of a former officeholder. If not, it *must* be a name that has been much in the news. Picking an alias is legally easy as long as you're not changing your name for fraudulent purposes. Winning elections is not a fraudulent purpose. A good political name is an absolute necessity. It can even disguise an ill-equipped candidate or elect one of no qualifications at all. Remember how easily Millard Fillmore Douglas and John Fitzgerald III were elected last year?

Your wife won't like the idea of changing her name again, just as she won't like your getting involved in politics. But you haven't been getting along with her very well anyway. She's always yapping about more children, and you disagree on how little George should be raised. Just because she once heard something in a college psychology course about frustrating children, she lets the baby run about like a home version of a bulldozer. When you contradict her, she doesn't even remember whether the professor thought permissiveness was good or bad, only that he mentioned it. She may be attractive, but she doesn't understand you the way your mother does.

Mother! If it weren't for the old man and his damn cribbage board, you'd spend a lot more time with your mother. She always has a rare roast of beef or something else nice to eat. And she listens to your problems while she's watching TV. Never mind. Escape all this.

RULE 2. *Replace your mother, wife or mistress with politics.*

The time you devote to your family is time away from politics. If there isn't somebody to see, there's somebody to call, or somebody seeing or calling

3

"Cravings for deference, frustrated or over-indulged in the intimate circle, find expression in the secondary environment."—*Politics: Who Gets What, When, How* by Harold D. Lasswell

you. In fact, if a day passes without your phone ringing busily, you've lost your support. If you can do nothing else at the beginning, go to the bar where the local pols hang out. Let them educate you.

If you'll let it, politics will solve your personal problems, be your security blanket, hold your hand, and make you a democratic royalist with the title Honorable. Whatever you can't find at home or in your mother's kitchen, politics will give you.

These first two rules are your tickets for first-class seats on the political rocket. If you can't follow them, take up needlepoint, you can't be a successful politician. If you accept them, you're ready to climb aboard.

You will? Then by the authority vested in this book, we hereby dub you politician with a capital P (Politician). You are endowed with all the powers and immunities of that exalted caste. You may make speeches, call officeholders by their first names, and tattoo "The greatest good for the greatest number" or "Politics is everybody's business" on your upper left arm. You're a Politician, and you're ready to blast off.

2

☒ Becoming part of a political organization

You need a political organization to power your moves to the top. As a Politician, you never refer to the organization as a machine. That's a word used by editorial writers, Young Turks, and Yahoos. To avoid any Freudian slips later, you should at this point repeat at least one hundred times:

> I'm a straight organization man.
> I'm a straight organization man.
> I'm a straight organization man.

Use the Regular Organization in your ward. Starting an organization of your own is not only troublesome and expensive, but it will brand you as a rump politician. That's not good. We want you to get ahead, not start behind. Therefore

RULE 3. *Join the minority party.*

A party is only temporarily out of power; sunken political ships bob up to sail again. If you get in when others are getting out, you'll be in on the salvage operation, and your reward will be a nice share of the treasure trove. Besides, the party in power has too many incumbents. Places on the ballot will be harder to snare. Incumbents can usually be displaced only by their deaths. Murder is not permitted, although provoking political suicide can usually be justified.

There is no real difference between parties. What we say here can be applied to either of them. But do be careful to remember the name of the party you join. It just won't do to make *that* kind of mistake.

Once you have selected your party, find out where the headquarters is, and learn as much as you can about the Ward Boss. Your next step is to make your first trip to the headquarters. But before you go, there are several things you must know.

A political headquarters is not intended for use by normal people. It's the command post from which the Boss deploys his troops. It's a private club and a legal loitery for the faithful, and often

a laundry for crying towels. It's a mess! You'll
have to step over beer cans, cigarette butts, out-
of-date sample ballots, and an overtired worker or
two. Don't be upset by your surroundings, you'll
soon begin to feel very comfortable in them.

The rooms of the headquarters require some de-
scription. The largest will be a meeting room.
You'll be able to recognize it by the presence of a
table and a large number of chairs. More chairs
than necessary give the impression of a large and
active organization. The pictures on the walls will
show the Boss shaking hands with other important
political personalities. Between the pictures—in
fact, wherever there are no pictures—there will be
graffiti—comments, sayings, unusual poems, and
the like. Make sure you read everything on the
walls. These scribblings are a valuable capsule history of who is who, and who was who in the party.
There's no hurry. The scribblings are an important
historical research source, so the walls will never
be repainted.

A large American flag, with a plaque beneath it
guaranteeing that it flew (momentarily) over the
United States Capitol, will identify the next to last
room in the headquarters—the Boss's office. Since
this room will look much the same as the rest of
the headquarters, only the flag and the sign "Please
Keep Out Unless Invited In   THIS MEANS YOU"
will distinguish it.

There is one other room and the door to it will

always be closed. That door says PRIVATE. Until much later in your political career you'll get little more than a peek into this room—the Favor Center. Here are one or more of the Boss's key accomplices who specialize in doing favors. In this room are processed the tickets to be fixed, the requests for street repairs, relief forms to be filled out, and other good deeds. You can't get in; only the Boss and his minions can. And there is some question whether those inside can get out.

In a corner of the hall there will be two younger men engaged in conversation. They'll be there no matter when you go to headquarters. You may think, at first glance, that they seem just the sort you'd like to be friendly with. They probably are. But they are discussing ideology and issues. Avoid them. They will have to be shunted aside later, so it's best never to get involved with them at all.

The center of all activity at the headquarters is the Boss himself. Whether sitting or standing he'll be partly surrounded by people. Partly—so that no one can get behind him. In the ward organization he's executive, magistrate, coordinator, personnel director, and switchboard operator. Most important, he's an overseer who directs the activities of his road gang. Chained to him by favors received or expected, they labor at his command. He has the power to make them, and never lets go of the power to break them. Like the progeny of a tiger mated to a canary, when he opens his mouth to

9

"No nation has ever believed more firmly that its political life was based on a perfect theory. And yet no nation has ever been less interested in political philosophy or produced less in the way of theory."—*The Genius of American Politics* by Daniel J. Boorstin

sing, they'd better listen.

The Boss is gracious and charming, and at home with people, especially those who submit to him completely. He'll admit he's liable to make a mistake, but he doesn't really believe it. Oh, he made one mistake back in '29, but he doesn't remember any since. His job pays no salary, but it does sometimes have earnings. That he has two or three tons of paper money in a closet at home is of no consequence. He may have a wealthy posterity, but he himself must always display the signs of his humble origins.

The Boss, you will learn, was born with hoof-and-mouth disease. Though inoculations have been tried, he is still galloping in all directions to keep his people happy and his organization effective. His mouth is a precise instrument that cajoles, wheedles, impresses, castigates, or invokes as needed.

With this knowledge as background, you're ready for your first visit to headquarters. Pick a night when it's fairly crowded. When you arrive, find the Boss and stand about twelve to fifteen feet away from him.

Don't approach the Boss directly. He's suspicious of anyone who volunteers, and will not react favorably if you appear to be too eager. Someone will notice you and ask who you are or what you want or both. Then say,

"Heard about this place. Just wanted to

drop around and see."

Note that you don't say what you heard or what you want to see. You have created an interest at least equal to the suspicion. That's the best you can do.

The member who has accosted you will break off the conversation and report immediately to the Boss, who will send him back to bring you over. As you walk toward him, let your eyes play on the Boss's pictures on the wall. Wear an expression of undisguised admiration. If you can't manage that, surprise will have to suffice.

The Boss will comment,

> "Nice to see you . . .?"
> "Small, sir. Franklin Pierce Small."
> "Any relation to Governor Small?"
> "My father used to speak of him, sir."

RULE 4. *Never answer a question directly.*

A direct answer pins you down to a position. Later, when you must deal with the press and citizens' groups, facility with the indirect answer will be important. But the technique must be absolutely perfect, so practice now on the less important things. The answer you gave is good because the Boss has an opportunity to believe whatever he wants.

> "What can we do for you, Small?"

He really wants to know what *you* can do for *him,* but he won't express that yet. He is also establishing that he is indeed the Boss, the man in a position to do things for you.

"I'd like to be a member of *your* organization. Thought I might help out in Eighteen, sir."

Don't tell him you know that there hasn't been a Captain in Eighteen for a year or more. That would imply he isn't able to run a good organization. That "help out" is important, too. You establish that you don't expect to start right at the top. Your humility will endear you to the party professionals later.

Now your position is stated, and the Boss will want to find out more about you. He has already observed your tailor-made suit and the Cadillac you drove up in. (These items are important. If you don't have them now, get them. You must be aware that there will be incidental expenses along the way.) He wants to know what you, personally, are after. This is the most important part of the interview.

"Had any experience?"
"I was in line for an office in the Wallabys, sir."

Don't tell him you *lost.* You want to establish yourself as a person with the right connections.

"Lived in the precinct long?"
"We know a lot of people there."

Good. A political Boss wants one thing from a worker, votes in the primary election. Votes are the only real measure of his organization's effectiveness and the standard of his power in Party gatherings. You've made him think that you might be able to get out a strong primary vote for the candidates he prefers.

"Might be able to put you in. Could have you work under Burnham here for awhile."

The Boss is not saying that you can't work alone; he's giving Burnham a pat on the back. Burnham needs to feel he's in. You'll never see him except at headquarters, and you will work the precinct alone. But don't let the Boss, or Burnham, know you realize this.

"Sounds like a real chance for me, sir."

Emphasize the *for me*. Bosses exist by doing things for others. By putting yourself in his debt, you have surrendered to him. This is what he's after. But you still have to allay some of his suspicions. He's not entirely sure yet that you don't want his brother-in-law's job in the Sewer Department.

You don't, incidentally. No matter what political jobs are offered to you, steadfastly refuse them. To accept a political job is to eliminate immediately any chance to be a candidate. You will build an obligation by successfully working the precinct, and this obligation will be repaid you at the lowest possible cost. Make sure the Boss understands that your motivation is not to get a payroll job. But don't tell him what you really want.

"Good Government is everybody's business, don't you agree?"

He doesn't. Good government is the concern of the party caucus. But the question keeps the conversation on a high level. Don't make it too high, though. Display immediately some of the selfish motivation he best understands.

"My company may want to do some government work next year."

That should do it. His brother-in-law's job is safe. He has visions of plentiful campaign contributions. And you have established yourself as an important man in the company. He won't make you a Precinct Captain officially until later, but you can be sure the job is yours. You're on your way.

☒ Bringing in the votes

Although you're now a Precinct Captain, you're not ready to go out into the hustings and begin beating about in search of votes. Nor will the Ward Boss think so. He'll suggest that you attend the training sessions held every Tuesday evening at headquarters. Since the sessions will be led by one of the useful, articulate ornaments of the Organization, it's important that you attend. It's equally important that you don't believe much of what you hear there.

The session leader is one of those people who believe that the Constitution was perfect at the time it was adopted and has improved since then, if only we'd stick to it. He thinks that people vote because the Precinct Captain convinces them that his party and his candidates are best for country, state, county, village, or humanity. They don't. People vote because their cousin knows a guy, because you sent a piece of flowers to the hospital, or because they expect to get a bigger pay, relief or social security check. The session leader, you will learn, tends to confuse what should be with what is.

When you go to the first session, next Tuesday, you won't find many people there. The Boss won't be there either. He's too busy getting things done to spend time discussing how they should be done. But your attendance will mark you as interested and willing to learn. As you enter, greet the session leader by his first name.

"Hi, Mark. I'm a bit early."

You're not early, of course, but saying so will put the session leader at ease, since there are only two other people there. And they are the two younger men who stand in a corner of the hall discussing ideology and issues. Avoid them again.

The session leader will begin talking the minute you arrive, and he won't run down for two or three hours. While he's talking

RULE 5. *Make many notes.*

Provide yourself with a small black notebook. At the training session it can be used for making notes on the subject covered, although it will probably be more valuable in juggling last week's expense account. Always keep the notebook with you. From time to time, at meetings, during conversations, or (sometimes) alone in a corner, scribble in it. You needn't write anything; doodling will have the desired effect. Of course, there will be certain essential information you'll want to record carefully.

As the session leader is talking, be sure to change expressions often. Surprise, concern, interest, admiration, if used judiciously, can save you the trouble of listening intently. The session leader is a rare political personality: he does not want to be President; he wants to be Chief Justice.

He'll say,

> "The majority party is doing everything wrong. Taxes are too high; schools are not good enough; the people are losing control of the government; our party is the only hope of mankind."

In fact, the majority party must be doing *something* right, or it wouldn't be the majority party. He'll continue,

> "The people have to be convinced that they are in trouble, and to do this we have to know the issues and have answers for all their objections."

Fine. But don't try to tell the plumber next door—

who has two cars and central air conditioning—that he is in trouble. You'll do better to tell him he'll be able to buy two new cars every year and air-condition his garage if he votes for your man.

"People," the session leader will insist, "are different now. The Precinct Captain can no longer serve their personal needs down to bread and coal. He must appeal to their new interest in the issues and the more complex concepts of government."

He's right. People are different now; they're less interested in politics. At the turn of the century, politics was a diversion. Now it is an intrusion. People don't want to be bothered with troublesome decisions, such as whom to vote for. So you help them. You make it possible for them to vote for you instead of for individual party candidates.

If you have a lot of spare time, you can ask a question at this session. It won't be answered, but it will give the leader a chance to talk even more, and you'll make a good impression. The leader will prate on in the same vein at every training session, maybe even in the same words.

Once you have been properly trained, it is time to begin working in the precinct, punching doorbells, as the less active workers in the Organization will say. Although it's important that you be successful in your first election, this success can be gained in different ways. You may even have to

19

call on voters.

If the circumstances are right, you can be very successful without wasting a lot of time on the people. The Boss will have at least one favorite candidate in the primary election you're working. He's selected this candidate for his ability as an officeholder, his past record, and—the number of jobs he has promised the Organization if he's elected. If the Boss has picked an Irish candidate and you live in a predominantly Irish precinct, then the job is partly done for you. If this candidate wins newspaper endorsements, throws an expensive TV campaign, or has a mother living in your precinct, your job is that much easier.

You realize, of course, that you must know the make-up of your precinct. In the first place, you'll have picked one with the same ethnic and religious background and financial circumstances as your own. Or at least the background and circumstances you reveal to the public. Later you will have to know the make-up of the district or even of the state. Then you can appeal individually to each group. You can never assume that any group is unimportant; if there's a Chinese laundry in the precinct, learn a few phrases of genuine Chinese.

When it's necessary to call on all the voters in your precinct, follow proven techniques. Call on people when it's convenient for them, not at the dinner hour, at nap time, or during a baseball game. Be polite. Never argue. In fact,

RULE 6. *Avoid talking politics in the precinct.*

When you work in the precinct, put your opinions in your briefcase and lock your briefcase in a closet. Your purpose is to gain votes, not to overwhelm voters with your rhetoric and logic. Therefore you must develop an approach based on reasonableness. There's a thin line between persuasion and argument, and it's not always possible to tell exactly when the line will be crossed. So don't persuade, influence. Never argue.

Most voters won't want to talk about the election. That would be asking them to make a decision. To decide, they have to think, to form opinions. And, after all, they're tired from a hard day at the office, plant, or whatever. Besides, they feel that what they do isn't important. As a result, some of them won't answer the bell at all. Others will keep the outer door closed, and your message will have to travel through a sheet of plate glass. But those you talk with will all be pleasant.

Beware of complainers. Those who complain the loudest, especially on big issues, are those who vote the least. And when they do vote, they always vote *against* something or someone. You must handle them gently. If you can imply that your candidate's opponent is the kind that causes the problems the voter is complaining about, you may score. But you would have to be very subtle; you should do little more than create a stirring of doubt about

21

the opponent.

A few voters will want to discuss the issues and the candidates. They'll state their positions on the election in a well-informed manner. You don't have to respond. Merely nod agreeably from time to time. If they are on your side, no problem. If not, after you have agreed a sufficient number of times, try,

> "You certainly put it well. Perhaps you'd like to discuss this with Ed White himself. I can arrange it for you."

Ed White is the candidate you're pushing, for the Boss, of course. The voter may never have mentioned him or his opponent. This makes no difference. Your suggestion that he express his opinions directly to a candidate will impress him. Take him to a rally at which Ed White is present and introduce them. Ed will be polite and listen. Your voter will be impressed with having been listened to, and he will vote for Ed. Never argue.

There will be some die-hards of the opposite party who will object to your existence. Remember to be agreeable. If the voter comes to the door with an oversized mastiff and greets you by suggesting that the beast

> "Kill!,"

respond, while protecting your jugular, with

> "Well trained, isn't he?"

Don't bother to prolong the discussion. Never argue.

Some voters are lonely. When you come around they'll want you to stay, perhaps for the weekend, and help break the monotony. They may talk about the election, but, more likely, the conversation will be about back home in Chillicothe. No matter. Stay only until you can easily break away. As you leave, say,

> "By the way, Ed White, the candidate for Sheriff? He's from Chillicothe."

You have a job to do. No matter how pleasant a visit may become, you have to get your pitch in and get away. Only in the case of young, attractive, lonely widows does the rule against arguing not apply.

You'll find many voters who are interested in certain aspects of the election or certain kinds of candidates. You can use that interest to help your own candidate. A copy of the *Daily Gzordia* lying on a table will prompt you.

> "Did you know that Ed White, the candidate for Sheriff, is a close friend of Stan Wojakowski?"

Stan, of course, is also a candidate. If you can do it successfully, suggest that Ed White's father changed his name. *Not* Ed, his *father*. Don't worry about finding a candidate with the right kind of

"America was meant to be everything. . . . There are many soils and many climates included within the boundary line of the United States; many *countries;* and one rule cannot be laid down for all."—Harriet Martineau

name. All modern party tickets are balanced. If there is a significant Egyptian settlement in your city, there will be an Egyptian candidate on the ballot. In fact, you can tell from, say, a county slate the proportions of the different ethnic groups in the community: if two out of ten candidates on the ballot are Outer Mongolians, then 20 per cent of the county are Outer Mongolians. Unfortunately, the proportions on the ballot were made up several years ago and may not reflect current shadings.

If the voter comes to the door wearing a cap with buttons showing he's paid his union dues for the past forty-two months, say,

> "Ed White's a good fellow, been a member of Local 617 for years."

Of course, you pick a local other than the one on the voter's hat. Never argue.

Framed certificates hanging on the wall of the voter's home may guide your approach. A voter who is a life member of the Audubon Protective League will react favorably to

> "Ed White plans on rigidly enforcing the law against plucking woodcock feathers to tie trout flies."

If this causes the husband of the house to bristle, add quickly,

> "Except under controlled conditions."

Never argue.

There are many other kinds of people. You can use these simple guidelines to develop approaches for each individual. But you must be wary. You may mistake agreeability with agreement. The voters will return your easy attitude with one of their own. Because they smile a lot, you may easily make the mistake of thinking that you have sold them. Not necessarily so.

Voters don't want to upset you. A man's brother may depend for a living on your candidate's opponent. But he won't tell you this. He'll nod, agree, look impressed, take your literature, and greet you warmly on election day. Then, in the privacy of the voting booth, he will vote the way he had intended from the beginning. To offset this problem you must work to develop a solid core of voters who will follow you . . . and only you.

For example, perhaps dear Mrs. Reilly has just had a baby, her tenth. Send Mrs. Reilly a potted plant in the hospital and a layette for the baby when she gets home. A bottle of his favorite elixir will do for Mr. Reilly. Then call on all the voters in the Reillys' block.

"I'm Frank Small, your new Precinct Captain. Was just over to the Reillys to see the new baby, thought I'd stop by here to get acquainted. Fine family the Reillys, and a beautiful baby it is now. A fine Irish family the

Reillys."

Usually, that's all you'll have to say. The people you're calling on will do the rest themselves. They'll be telling you what a fine family they themselves are, and will probably trot out the youngest or prettiest or smartest of their brood. At crucial points, venture a comment:

> "Ah, but it's fortunate you are."
> "Why, she's the image of Shirley Temple."
> "Only eight you say. Why he looks to be twelve."

You should genuinely like children. Though untidy little beasts, they do grow up to be voters.

As you leave, after having had a drop of the "creetur," say,

> "I'd appreciate your giving my good friend Ed White a vote in next Tuesday's election. He's running for the Sheriff job. Ed comes from a fine family, eleven children."

After all the conversation about fine families, it's an appeal that can't miss. You've gotten not only the Reillys, but some of their neighbors as well. Don't forget to send the same things to the neighbors as you did to the Reillys when the neighbors have a baby. You've as much as promised to do so.

Another effective technique is to become friendly with the neighborhood druggist or florist. They usually know who's on the disabled list. You can then call on the sick, sore, lame, and injured at just the right time. But the best of all vote-getting methods is waking the dead.

Understand, we don't mean just going to the wakes of demised voters in your precinct. You must, to do the job properly, wake the parents, children, aunts, uncles, cousins, and very close friends of the people in your precinct. Of necessity, therefore, you must be comfortable at wakes of all religions and all kinds. If the rabbi chants, you chant. If the priest prays, you pray. If possible, be a pallbearer. They're your people from the cradle to the grave.

Build your solid core by making the right appointments. You have two or three spots for election judges that you can fill. Technically, these positions are appointed by an election authority, but, in practice, the Ward Boss sends in the names you suggest. You will suggest people who can control votes. An election judge from a family with five votes is a suitable appointment.

On election day you will need checkers, watchers, and a variety of standers. They will be paid from the allowance you will receive for this purpose (see Chapter 6). They, too, should be selected on the basis of the number of votes they can bring in. They should also have a job to do. The standers might, for example, pass out sample ballots or slices of homemade strudel to voters as they come to the polls.

Work 365 days a year to develop your core into a sizeable group. As it grows, your own legwork will lessen, and you'll become more and more valuable to the organization. Do for them before someone else does. Be nice to children, help old ladies cross the streets, hire a tractor to plow the snow from the sidewalks. Do favors whenever you can, and make a careful record of them in your black notebook.

You're an important man to your people. For the most part, you're their only link with government and politics. Government, incidentally, is merely politics from the winners' point of view. You'll help them fill out the forms and see that they get what they justly deserve from the government. All you ask in return is that they spend their votes as you suggest, a small enough price. After all, your motives are completely unselfish. You want to give them the benefit of your ability as Governor.

A successful record as a Precinct Worker is the *sine qua non* of the Organization Politician. If effort is needed to bring in a favorable vote, make it. Young presidents of corporations and sons of billionaires may skip this step. But if you aren't one or the other, you must take the rougher road through the precinct. Your success will mark you as a valuable member of the Ward Boss's team, and he'll want you as much as you want him.

4

⊠ Becoming a statesman

You, Franklin Pierce Small, successful precinct worker, are now ready for elective office. But which office? True, one must start at the very bottom, and you did. Fortunately, rungs can be skipped on the way up.

RULE 7. *Run for the highest office to which you can be elected.*

Be careful here. It's foolish to run for Governor the first time out if you cannot be elected. It's equally foolish to run for Sanitation Supervisor if you can be elected to a higher office. Normally, assuming you have the good sense to live in a district that is safe for your party, your first outing should be for the state legislature. You want an office that is as far away from the people as possible.

Local offices are among the worst choices. Not only are many of them nonpaying, but also, from time to time, the people become annoyingly interested in local affairs. Although this doesn't happen often by any means, many fine political careers are ruined when it does. It's frightening how civic-minded some people can become after blowing a tire in a chuckhole on East Fourth Street. Don't take the chance.

It's also desirable to keep the line to your goal as direct as possible. County and federal offices, while fulfilling the requirement of being away from the people, at least from the standpoint of interest, are not in a direct line to the Governorship. They, too, present risks. People know more about their Congressman than they do about their state legislators. County offices are the object of occasional inquiry.

So the state legislature is the perfect place to start. Sessions are not held often enough to interfere with your important political activities. They are usually held away from your city. And, best of all, most voters have no knowledge of or interest in what you do in the legislature—except at election time or in a few other instances which we will mention later.

Of course, since yours is a safe district, the incumbents will have been in office for a long time.

This is to your advantage, if you handle matters well. What you must do is create a vacancy and be sure that you are the one chosen to fill it. This is not as difficult as it may seem.

Grasp first this essential: Politicians never retire; they always envision themselves in higher office. The easiest way to move an officeholder out is up. To make a place on the ballot for yourself as State Senator, then, you must plant a seed and see that it germinates and comes to bloom.

Cultivate the incumbent State Senator. You know his favorite bar, and you have visited him there many times. Then, at exactly the right moment, when he is alone in the bar—he should have been there long enough to be receptive, but not long enough to be unconscious—plant your seed. Broach the subject just after he's completed one of his stories on how much he's done for the party, the state, and the voters.

"Senator, your talent really suits you to higher office. Why are they holding you back?"

He agrees that he's a natural for higher office. But this is the first he's heard that somebody is holding him back. He'll answer,

"The legislature is pretty important,"

He's rationalizing, of course. He'd really like one of the clerical offices, such as State Auditor. Most

"A rayformer thries to get into office on a flyin' machine. He succeeds now an' thin, but the odds are a hundred to wan on th' la-ad that tunnels through."—Mr. Dooley

of the Auditor's decisions can be made by comput-
er, and those that can't are deputized to an assistant. After ten years in the legislature, he's tired of
making decisions. You have sown your seed. Now
cover it with a thin layer of topsoil.

"You'd certainly have my support."

To be sure that your seed germinates, have
twenty or more friends write letters to the Senator,
telling him that a man of his fiscal integrity is
needed as State Auditor. (At least one letter should
mention the word "Governor" so that he'll begin
thinking about the step after State Auditor.)

Soon after, at ward headquarters, ask a party
regular stuck with a low-paying patronage job if
he's going to work for the Senator after he becomes
State Auditor. Word will get around that the Senator is running and that there will be several jobs
available for the organization. This will put the
Senator in a position from which he cannot retreat,
and it will force the Boss to support him or appear not to have adequate control of his organization or sufficient interest in providing his workers
with the positions they deserve. If you can fertilize
your seed with a campaign contribution for the
candidate for Auditor, so much the better. Make it
an anonymous contribution.

Now, to reap the harvest you have so carefully
sown, you must be sure you are selected to run for
the State Senate in place of the incumbent. Here

you need an advocate, a Political Wheel with greater power than your own Boss. The perfect choice is the Chairman of the Screening Committee. A screening committee is a powerful group that suggests candidates to the Party. If it's the usual sort of Screening Committee, mere suggestion is sufficient. The Chairman's position makes him not only valuable but easy to approach. He wants candidates who will be amenable to the suggestions he'll make from time to time.

Develop an intimacy with your Political Wheel, using the same techniques you used to cultivate the Senator. Here admiration will not be enough. Only an absolute dependence on him will suffice. For example, you must constantly ask his advice on political matters. And follow that advice if possible. It doesn't matter whether the deference you show is real as long as it seems to be. The Political Wheel you have thus encircled will get the support of the Ward Boss for you.

As Chairman of the Screening Committee he'll call the Ward Boss on some pretext that will take up most of the conversation. Toward the end of the call he'll say,

> "I understand there's a good chance for coalition in the judicial election. We may have to call on you to serve. I thought I'd recommend you to the rest."

The Boss's reaction to this suggestion is an orgy

of physical emotion. His salivary glands flow, his gastric juices gurgle. His eyes widen to the point of assuming a life of their own, and his adrenal glands function at an all-time high. To be a coalition candidate is to be elected, since the parties cooperate to nominate only the number of candidates necessary to fill the vacancies available. The Boss wants to be a judge.

At the right moment the Political Wheel exacts his price for the judgeship.

"By the way, understand you're going to run the Senator for State Auditor. Good idea. Have you thought of a candidate for his spot?"

The Boss may not have been sure the Senator was a candidate. The Political Wheel's statement makes it official. While the Boss has a few names in mind, he knows what's going on. Since he wants to be a judge, he says,

"There are several good people in my organization. Did *you* have anyone in mind?"

He knows the Political Wheel does, but he's protecting his flanks by saying "several people" and not naming any.

"Frank Small seems to me to be a good man for the job."

The Wheel has put it on such a basis that the Boss can only say,

"Well, some others have been around longer, but Small has caught on pretty quick."

That's no understatement. Anyone who can get the support of the Chairman of the Screening Committee has damn well caught on pretty quick.

There are some formalities left. First the Screening Committee must select you. Then the Nominating Convention must ratify your selection. Even though you have been picked by the Boss and the Chairman of the committee, it will still be necessary for you to appear before the full Screening Committee. This is a group which takes minutes and wastes hours to give the impression that the Chairman is not an autocrat.

You need not worry about questions from the committee members. Many will be asked; only two are important.

"Have you ever run for a political office and lost?"

Politicians, like criminals, are judged by the number of times they have been losers.

Since the Chairman, to protect his public image, can never *demand* cash, the second important question is:

"You know, Small, that each candidate is expected to do his share. The assessment this year is two thousand dollars. If you are picked, are you prepared to pay?"

"Yes, sir. Immediately, in cash."

Note the *immediately* and *in cash*. Political organizations do not take IOU's in payment of assessments. Installment plans are still being studied.

Your answer to the last question will be the signal for the Committee to adjourn. The handshaking and whomps on the back are a sign that you are soon to become a member of that select club, the Party Slate.

You are the candidate, but you will and must be officially invested with the title. This will be done at a convention. Simply defined, conventions are gatherings of party leaders met to endorse the decisions already made by more powerful party leaders. Although they are held at many levels, the one of interest to you is that which will nominate you as a candidate for State Senator. This convention may be attended by leaders from your Senatorial District, or it may be of leaders from the entire county. Whichever hardly matters: the conventions are all the same.

Political conventions are much like business conventions. The official portions are considerably less important than the extracurricular activities. More than likely, the convention will be held in a large hotel. As a prospective candidate, you will be expected to provide a "hospitality suite." This is little more than a transference of the functions of the hotel's restaurant and beverage facilities to your rooms. This gives the delegates the chance to meet you, discuss important issues, and avoid spending their own money.

The actual nominating session will take place in one of the numerous rooms the hotel has for the purpose. These rooms, named after generals of the Spanish-American War or riverboats long drowned in the Mississippi, are all the same. The one pattern, drawn in 1903, has never been changed. Decorated in a colloidal mixture of British Guiana rococo and Lebanese provincial, the room has many chairs and a microphone. Maybe a table with a podium. An inefficient ventilation system guarantees that the proper atmosphere will be maintained. There may be a small room within the meeting room designed to facilitate the dispensing of coffee and the like. There is also a place provided to enable the press to attend closed sessions. This may be the coffee room or it may be nothing more than a closet divided off by a curtain eight inches shorter than it should be.

If the meeting is small enough, coffee will be provided for early arrivals. Actually, nobody comes early, but the schedule says "for early arrivals." One of the delegates who has come in after his absence was noted by the secretary may ask,

"Mr. Chairman, is there any coffee left?"

The chairman will confer with his close advisors and answer in the affirmative. The delegate will then ask,

"Mr. Chairman, where the ——— are the ——— rolls?"

Another conference around the podium.

"We're sorry, but the delegate from the Forty-second Ward missed roll call."

And so it proceeds.

Your Political Wheel, as Chairman of the Screening Committee, will also be the Chairman of this meeting. The Boss will nominate you, or see to it that you are nominated by someone in his organization. Then real unity is achieved. The Chairman begins to call on other leaders to second your nomination. These leaders don't know you. They may not have known you were to be nominated. They certainly did not know they were to be called on. But each of them will extoll to all within earshot, which may be a considerable distance, the advantages you offer as a candidate. Don't begin to feel too good. They say the same thing at every meeting and for every candidate.

5

⊠ Petitions

Although you are supported by the Organization, since you live in a safe district, you can expect another candidate to oppose you in the primary election. Somebody who doesn't know the rules will think he can beat you.

The direct primary, which pits party members against each other, is a biennial bloodletting that was designed by reformers around the turn of the century to do away with politicians. With their usual adaptability the politicians soon came to achieve the same results with the primary as they did before it. They merely moved the selection process from large, smoke-filled convention halls to small, smoke-filled hotel rooms.

Before you actually begin your campaign, your

name must appear on the ballot. To get it there you must file nominating petitions signed by voters from your district. These petitions are the politician's answer to the direct primary laws. The difficulty of securing the large number of signatures usually required keeps the ballot from being cluttered up with independent candidates. Organizations are experienced in completing petitions; reformers aren't.

Basically, there are two ways to gather the names you need. We recommend the more difficult of the two. It's legal. The second method is presented here for information only. It should be used only in an absolute emergency, such as a nuclear attack.

The first name-getting technique is to collect signatures directly from the voters. Obviously this can be done most quickly where there are large groups of people gathered, such as at church affairs or at cocktail parties. At both, people will be receptive to a suggestion that they are doing their civic duty by signing. They will also be less apt to ask questions, since there will be little opportunity for serious discussion. Merely say,

"Will you please sign my nomination for Senator?"

Don't call it a petition, or they'll think you're for one-way streets or something. Give them a chance to be good citizens without worrying about results.

Do not pass the petition from pew to pew at

church (or at cocktail parties either, for that matter). You may lose control of it and never see it again. And since these signers may be molders of opinion, personal contact at this time will win their support during the campaign. Most of them have never met a Senator before.

To get maximum exposure at a church, have the clergyman announce,

"All good citizens are requested to leave by the Main Street exit."

This will assure that most of the people will pass your station there. If you can, stand next to the pastor, or have him be the first signer. (Arrangements with the pastor are in your hands. This is not a book on religious doctrine.)

Two hours after the fourteenth guest has arrived has been shown by science to be the best time for petition signing at cocktail parties. Then people are most friendly—and still able to write. Of course, you will not be drinking, for someone has to see that the petition sheets are not used for coasters or paper airplanes. Incidentally, don't use women's backs as a desk. Ballpoint pens make marks on bare backs, and the ladies will leave looking as though they'd been tattooed.

If you cannot obtain signatures in any other way, you can resort to the round table. Understand, we are referring to a technique, not to furniture. Gather six to twelve friends, an assortment of pens, and a phone directory or polling list. Each person signs a name from the list and passes the petition to his right. The next person does the same. And so on. This method is quick, effective—and illegal. If you say we recommended it, we'll deny it.

Once you have collected the signatures, you must file them. Don't stop at filing them in the way the statutes prescribe.

RULE 8. *Always get first place on the ballot.*

This may be the most important rule in the book. Voters fall generally into three classes: the ignorant, the indifferent, and the uninformed. Relax. We're not suggesting that you run out and try to educate the ignorant, arouse the indifferent, or enlighten the uninformed. Others have tried and failed. You can achieve better results by being first on the ballot for your office.

People vote because it is their duty. But except for such offices as President or U.S. Senator, who they vote for is purely accidental. First place on the ballot is always likely to benefit from these accidents. You may hear talk of some malcontents who are voting for candidates from the bottom up. Don't worry about them. Their crusade will be as successful as building a house from the chimney down.

To get first place on the ballot you must roll out your Political Wheel once again. He'll gladly do

"The Great American political chieftans without exception have had to be astute opportunists free from petrified ideas, and expediency has accordingly been the key to their party practices."—*American Political Parties: Their Natural History* by Wilfred E. Binkley.

you the favor, since it will make you even more amenable to some suggestions he'll make from time to time. He knows the speakeasy door, open only to initiates, where petitions are filed before the legal filing date. Of course, you realize there is a difference between the statute election laws and the real election laws. Petitions are a prime example of this difference.

The laws say that places on the ballot are awarded according to the order in which petitions are received. The statute laws. Politicians have devised a more complex, but much fairer, method of determining whose name goes where.

The clerk or secretary who receives the ballots holds a meeting the night before the filing day. He invites to his office certain key individuals in his party and perhaps a nonobjectionable representative of the other party. Your Political Wheel will be a member of this ad hoc committee. It is this committee, and not the vagaries of the clock, that determines positions on the ballot.

The committee follows certain well-defined patterns to decide who goes where. For example, incumbents with the longest service are usually given preferred positions. Close friends of members of the committee receive similar treatment. Members of regular organizations are placed above rump candidates who don't fit into either of the first two categories. Sometimes there are problems.

"Mr. Secretary, you have to give first spot

to Art. I promised him."

A valid reason, but the secretary may have one of his own.

"Art, hell! Sam. He helped me push through the State Police Expansion Bill."

Another factor in the decision is where to place candidates with strength who are opposing those preferred by the committee. If possible, their names are lost. But usually they are shown after everybody else. If there are enough candidates, they will be in the middle.

Sometimes even the secretary will have trouble deciding. For example, there is the case of two incumbents with equal service who must fight for one seat because of redistricting. The secretary has his own method of solving such problems. After all, he's paid to make decisions. And he and the ad hoc committee are dedicated public servants. They labor far into the night to see that poorly written laws do no harm.

If you're tempted to try to find the secret door by yourself, forget it. You probably won't. Even if you did, they wouldn't let you in. In any case, they know a fellow who for $25 will break your knee-cap with an iron bar. Let your Political Wheel help you along.

You must see by now that election laws are almost as effective as the Volstead Act. You're learning. It's time to start your primary campaign.

6

⊠ Campaign finances

Campaigns are always expensive. You do not have to be wealthy yourself; that comes later, after you are elected. You can trade on the experience of others to make fund-raising easy. Don't plan to get the money from your friends; you'll be disappointed. Also be wary of large contributors; their purposes are not noble. When you set your campaign budget,

RULE 9. *Plan to collect more money than you think you need.*

You always need more money than you think. Little things keep coming up. For example, if matters are going well, you may have to print fifty

48

thousand flyers at the last minute to answer a particularly vicious charge made by your opponent. Or, if things are going badly, to make a vicious charge against him. The money left over after your campaign can be used for those incidental expenses we discussed earlier. If you buy a new Cadillac, however, make sure it's the same color as the one you're now driving.

Your Ward Boss has no trouble raising funds, since there are candidates and job holders dependent on him. You cannot use his methods, but you can use his organization. You'll find that his workers are expert ticket sellers, so you should plan an affair involving the sale of tickets to raise funds.

Two such affairs of proven effectiveness are the Golf Day and the Theatre Party. In either case, the tickets sell for ten dollars, and with skillful planning you can keep most of the receipts. But understand that you do have to have the affair. Some people will want their money's worth.

Golf Day, or Franklin Pierce Small Day as it will be called, is the most used fund-raising device. You will probably select this gambit unless you happen to live in one of those rare wards that has an average literacy above fifth-grade level. By its nature the Golf Day will attract a predominently male audience, thus having the additional advantage over the Theatre Party of not shocking the ladies with the explicit language usually used by Politicians.

At the Golf Day the largest net profit will be

realized from golf itself, or, rather non-golf, since many people don't play. You then won't have to part with the greens fees. If you can pick a day when the sky is overcast and threatening rain, so much the better. And pick a day of the week, say Tuesday, when most men have to work. Thus can you keep the golfers down but the dinner attendance up.

Since the Day is in your honor, your political prestige will be enhanced by a large attendance. No one will ask what you are being honored for, so you needn't worry about having an answer ready.

Most of those who attend will be pols, or people on the fringes of politics who want to get in. Some few will actually play golf, thereby indicating that they are either real novices at politics or voters doing their civic duty. The pros won't play golf, except at the bar. And there they will seldom shoot under par. They are not there to engage in sport. It's a business day for them, and they'll spend it cultivating, reaffirming, or character assassinating.

Be sure to distribute a large number of prizes. The cost of the prizes can be kept to a minimum by having the members of the Organization harass local merchants with whom they do business. Merchants expect this and provide for it in their budgets. It's written off to shoplifting.

As you, and you must, distribute the prizes, use the opportunity to accolade the winners. Of course you'll see that the important people, among others, win prizes. This will give you a chance to say nice things about them. If you don't know them all, have the Boss or one of his people stand near you to identify them and help you say the right things.

> "Oh. Here's Ed Walsh's name. Ed wins a 96-cup teapot. Great job you're doing over there in the suburbs, Ed. You got a tough district."

The distribution of prizes is the climax of the evening. As a result, you can make utmost use of the time. Nobody will mind how long you talk . . . as long as there are prizes left. Some of the winners may be lubricating their sore muscles at the nineteenth hole by that time, but say something nice about them anyway. Someone else will tell them about it later. They'll also tell them if you don't say something nice.

You need not have prizes at a theatre party. People receive their money's worth by seeing the show. But here, too, a larger profit will be realized by keeping the attendance down. First, of course, you must sell considerably more tickets than there are seats in the theatre. If you select a theatre far from your area, near a railroad or airport, showing a play that most people have seen four or five times, you will have ample seats for those who actually come. The theatre has already provided sufficiently uncomfortable accommodations—you

51

need not worry about that. As insurance, you may arrange to have the movie version of the play shown on the local TV station the night before your affair.

These methods assure you more than adequate funds. But you should use the funds judiciously. Immediately after placing orders with printers and other suppliers, send them a check in partial payment of your account. You will thereby show them that you are a good credit risk. Some may even demand this. And after the initial payment it is unnecessary to pay them anything until after you are elected. At that time you'll find many of them will be more receptive to talk of discounts and reductions.

Printing and other similar expenses are secondary in the primary campaign. Your most important expenditure will be precinct money, a stipend provided the captains to help them defray their expenses. It seems that the more votes a captain produces, the higher his expenses will be, and thus the more precinct money he will receive.

Some of a captain's expenses are dinner for election judges, salary for poll watchers, or a weekend at a lakeside resort for himself and his wife. Precinct money should always be paid about a week before the election, and always in cash. It is not necessary to provide worn bills of small denominations in plain unmarked packages. The captains are no fools.

"Political Gifts tend to be regarded by many persons as the purchase of a lien on a candidate. . . ."—*Politics, Parties and Pressure Groups* by V. O. Key, Jr.

With sufficient money and the Organization's backing, you are assured of a good chance of success in the primary election. There are, however, ways to be absolutely sure of victory.

7

☒ Keeping the workers working

Because you are the Organization candidate for State Senator, your victory in the primary election depends not on you but on the Organization's workers. Therefore your efforts will be spent, for the most part, keeping them content. You needn't worry about jealousy. They may wonder why you were selected over them, but the fact that the Boss refers to you as "Senator" has sufficient finality to still their wonderings.

Besides the members of the Organization, you will have to accumulate a number of personal workers. This is not difficult to do, but there are a few pitfalls and types to avoid.

RULE 10. *Recruit your workers from people who expect something from you.*

Those who expect something know they can't get it until you're elected. So they'll work hardest to see that you are elected. Promise them whatever they want. Although in politics your word is your bond, you can't be expected to remember everything.

Workers are of two completely different kinds—men and women. A male candidate, like yourself, can handle the men all right, but you will need help in directing the women. The best helper is your wife.

Although your wife was against your entrance into politics, now she has changed. Her neighbors' constantly talking about you, the calls for "Senator Small," and other ego builders have brought her around. Besides, she'll have realized by this time that it's the only way she'll be able to see you regularly.

Don't spring things on her all at once. Be subtle. Don't, for example, say,

"I'm having phone jacks put into the house because of all the phone calls you're going to have to handle."

Instead, say,

"I'm having phone jacks put in so you won't have to walk so far to the phone."

If she notices the jack in the bathroom, just tell her there was an extra one and you didn't know where else to put it.

Next, have someone tell you, in her presence, that your opponent is charging she is the real power in the household. She'll think others feel she's playing a more important role than she is, and she will feel guilty. From this point on you can assume that she is one of your most avid workers. Don't tell her yet you're going to be Governor. You'll have enough expenses without buying her a new wardrobe. That will come later.

The Ward Boss does not like women in politics. To him they were God's first mistake. He has only partly reconciled himself to the blunder of the women's suffrage amendment. When you tell him that your wife is working with you, he'll be glad it's you and not him.

With your wife in the fold, you can proceed to have her recruit workers. She will use a simple approach. Her husband is running for Senator because he wants to reduce taxes, build better schools, regulate diaper service, or eliminate the sales tax on bridge cards. All these are reasons that excite women. They will believe that these are the real reasons you are running for office. And they will see that it is their civic duty to help you.

Among the women you'll find the following are the most helpful:

The Frowzy Frail. Despite the rundown heels

"Allons, enfants de la patrie,
Le jour de glorie est arrivé!
Contre nous de la tyrannie
L'étendard sanglant est levé!"
—*La Marseillaise* by Rouget de Lisle

and Good Will dress, she is the most useful of the flock. She'll work day and night, expecting little reward. Be sure to say something nice to her from time to time.

"Gina, you're worth five men to me" is recommended.

The Grapevine Grandmother. Her phone bill is larger than her food budget, but she can be useful if she's saying the right things. Tell her early in the campaign that your opponent favors vivisection. The word will soon spread all over the district, and his denials will fall on deaf ears.

The Civic Cutie. She's awfully, awfully interested in politics, don't you know? She speaks profoundly on the issues and questions all the commas in your printed material. Let your wife deal with her exclusively.

The Handy Heifer. She doesn't talk much, but is willing to run out for ice cubes or cigarettes at any time. There will be moments when she seems to be distracted. Don't bother her, she's bachelor-watching.

Most women are willing and helpful. Your wife will have little trouble with them, and you need do nothing more than praise them sincerely to keep them going.

Your wife's group of volunteers will be invaluable in helping you contact all the party voters in your district, especially the stamp lickers. The men you must recruit yourself. It is not a good idea for your wife to ask them for their services.

Among the men you'll need are:

A Speech Writer. You need only two speeches, and you'll find them in the Appendices. But you should have a speech writer, because all politicians with a future have them. Find an alert young college graduate who has a master's degree in history or English. The degree doesn't matter. It's more important that it be from one of the "right" schools. To recruit him, all you have to do is imply that you are going to be Governor. He will expect to be taken along to the mansion.

A Public Relations Man. Get a professional. You may even have to pay him, but he will be well worth it. The least he'll be able to do is deliver the endorsement of one of the major newspapers, and that is worth its weight in money.

An Aide. This is the male counterpart of the *Handy Heifer.* He'll be used for all the things that no one else wants to do. If your district warrants it, have two aides. Keep them with you at all times. Good aides can often be recruited by cultivating the Chairman of the Parole Board.

With a full complement of personnel, you have only one other problem to handle before the campaign itself. Preparing your home. You'll need about four rooms more than you now have. One way to solve the problem is to let the bedroom furniture stay with friends until the end of the campaign. You won't need it anyway.

Provide a briefing room for Precinct Captains. They are great worriers and will have a lot of little problems they must personally talk with you about. Use the briefing room for such consultations. A small refrigerator and an adequate supply of setups are all the furnishings needed. Chairs are merely an invitation to them to stay longer, when they should be out working for you.

You'll also need a communications center. But don't put in a switchboard, or your campaign will seem too organized. The communications center should be furnished with a large table and numerous chairs. Here letters addressed to voters will be processed. Sponges are recommended over tongues for sealing envelopes. They are replaceable.

Your regular furniture will be enough for the rest of the house if precautions are taken. Hide the silver. Install cheap carpeting over your better material. The cheaper stuff will be worn through by the end of the campaign and can then be discarded. Anchor all chairs. (One candidate lost the election because he installed an electric sign that lit up with the world "TILT" whenever anyone leaned back in a chair. Be more subtle.)

With these preparations completed, you're ready for the campaign.

8

⊠ **Winning the primary**

"And now, ladies and gentlemen, the next Senator from the Eighteenth District Franklin Pierce Small. Frank . . ."

Get used to this introduction. It's the one you'll hear at every meeting or rally you attend as a candidate. Politicians assume election well before it is a fact. And if they lose, they wear the title they sought long after the election. You're now Senator Small Fits you well.

Rallys and meetings will take most of your time during the primary campaign. The people there are not voters; but they are those to whom the voters will look for guidance, the Precinct Workers. As we have said, you must have this group on your side. It's true that the Organization behind you will assure your victory, but you want to be Governor. You have to win big. So you must get the workers really enthusiastic about you. One way to do this is

RULE 11. *Always make short speeches to party members.*

This will endear you to them as much as doubling their precinct money. Well, almost as much. Use the speech in Appendix I at all Party gatherings. All you really have to show is that you speak American. You can tell them nothing they haven't heard often before. Use the tried, true and short.

Another part of your presentation at Party meetings is to acknowledge the presence of every other candidate. Say something nice, even if you have to work at it. They will say the same about you, and it gives a nice feeling of solidarity. If you have trouble, practice the following:

> "I'm glad to see my dedicated, dear, dynamic friend [always insert a name] here tonight. His election will do a lot for the [country, state, county, or, if you don't know the office he's running for, the American Way of Life]. I, Franklin Pierce Small, heartily recommend to you [candidate] for the office of [name it]."

You'll think of other high praise as you go along.

Never use the same one more than twice at the same meeting, and mention your own name and the office you want as often as possible. Save your longest and warmest praise for the Boss of the Organization you're visiting. Everyone else will do the same; if you don't, he'll think you are part of a conspiracy to unseat him.

RULE 12. *Call people by name.*

To greet a Captain, especially one from another organization, by his first name is to add 10 per cent to your voting strength in his precinct. You don't have to learn all the names, though. There isn't time for that.

Many Organizations, being politically wise, provide their members with name tags to wear. Use them judiciously. Don't ever look straight at a name tag. Sneak a peak, then walk away. Before you forget the name, turn and walk up to the Captain, hand outstretched.

> "I'm Frank Small, Bob. Hope you'll be on my team."

Since you looked him right in the eye, he won't think of the name tag until much later. You will have produced the effect you want.

If the Organization you're visiting is politically immature and doesn't provide name tags, you will have to rely on eavesdropping. Stand where you

"It is a common American Fallacy to conclude that when a constitutional amendment, or a statute, or a charter, is secured the victory has been won and that the patriotic citizen may go back to the neglected plow."—*Primary Elections* by Charles E. Merriam

can hear more than one conversation. As soon as a name is mentioned anywhere, use it in the same manner as those you get from name tags.

Short speeches and names are good, but a sure-fire way to excite the Captains is to give them something extra. For example, before the primary there will be several one-hundred-dollar-a-plate dinners. Usually these affairs are not completely sold out . . . at a hundred dollars. The last few days before the dinner any tickets remaining are available for ten dollars each, maybe less if the advance sale is very bad. Of course, they still show the original price.

Buy up a bunch of these cut-rate tickets. When you're meeting the members of other Organizations, use them.

"Jim [remember that name tag], here's a couple of tickets to the Governor's Dinner on me. We especially want you to be there."

You've got him. He may even vote for you twice himself.

Don't make the mistake of buying the cut-rate tickets for yourself. You go first class. Incidental expenses again. As a candidate, you'll have to suffer through many dinners before you get a chance to talk a little. Use the speech in Appendix I. But, for heaven's sake, don't eat anything. You'll be at these dinners several times a week. There are some ailments modern medicine cannot cure.

With the party workers in the district well in tow, you can look forward to a sweeping victory in the primary election. Since you're in a safe district, the primary is enough. You need do little more than observe the formalities of campaigning to win in the general election.

Congratulations! You're now Franklin Pierce Small, Senator from the Eighteenth District.

9

⊠ **Life as a senator**

With your new title firmly affixed to your name, you're ready to take the next step toward the Governor's mansion, making a name for yourself as a Senator. This will be easy if you follow our rules. However, since your new colleagues do not know that you are going to be Governor, you must obey their rules first.

As a Senator now, you're a Wheel in your local Organization. Before you ran, a fellow Captain might ignore you or, at the most, greet you,

"Hi Frank, nice to see you."

As State Senator, you will gain his respect,

"Good evening, Senator. How are you?

How's your lovely wife? Terrific campaign you ran. We're lucky to have someone like you to work for."

Of course, you realize that his new attitude is based on more than the resonance of your title. As a Senator, you are a power in the Organization. You have the Boss's ear. The Boss has the power to vise the Captain. He doesn't want to be vised.

"Vising"? That's what the Boss uses to keep his people in line. Suppose a Captain has a job with the county. He reports to work at noon, takes an hour for lunch and quits at three. For which he is paid eighty dollars a week. Of course, he has a "regular" job too, but he's used to that extra eighty dollars. He wants to keep it. If he becomes difficult, in any way, all the Boss need do is call the Chairman of the County Board and tell him there is another man better qualified for that job. New qualifications are never questioned. The erring Captain is out. He's been vised.

There are other reasons for his new-found admiration of you. You may be in a position to do something for him. He isn't really sure of what, but if anything does come along, he wants to be sure you'll be willing to help.

The respect of your former peers is one of the reasons you want political success. But no matter how high you may go, there's always someone to whom you must pay homage. The Ward Boss, for example, although not as submissively as before.

Others are the Political Wheel and the State Auditor who held your Senate seat before you. But the largest group now are the senior Senators.

You're a freshman Senator, so nearly all are your seniors. They know the ins and outs of the State Capitol, the people who are important and the way to influence them. You'll be expected to play the same role here as you did when you were an Assistant Precinct Captain, quietly listening as they educate you.

You will ride to the first session of the Legislature in a parlor car. It's expected, and valuable too. All of the important members will be there. As you enter the car, take a seat near a Senator you recognize. With your head slightly bowed, and in a soft voice,

"I'm Frank Small. Honored to meet you, Senator."

A small choke or quiver in your voice is desirable. Use his title, not yours. You need say nothing more. He'll relieve you of the problem. And he will introduce you to the others in the car. This gives you a head start over other freshmen.

One of the topics in the car will be who is going to be the new President Pro Tem of the Senate. This is decided well before the caucus of the parties for the purpose, and learning now will be useful. Other intelligence will come to light also, if you are very quiet. From time to time slip away to the men's room (they will understand) and jot down essential information in your notebook.

When you are settled in the capital, begin making the rounds of the local bars. After a night and morning, you will know who goes where. Make notes in case you have to contact another Senator at any time. Legislative chambers are used because it is custom, but most business is conducted in the taverns.

You will be introduced at the party caucus. Resist the temptation to make a speech, even the one in Appendix I. Freshman Senators, like little children, are to be seen and not heard. Your vote on whom the party will support for President is important. You know who it is going to be and can vote for him early. Before the voting, go up to the candidate who will be President.

"Senator, I'm certainly glad you've made yourself available for the Presidency. We need you."

He'll know you know how the land lays, and it will help you to get a better seat in the Senate chamber.

Seats in the chamber are chosen in order of seniority. Your remark to the new President will enable you to be among the first freshman to have their names pulled from the hat.

RULE 13. *Sit near a Senate hero.*

Select a man who is praised by the newspapers and civic groups and consulted by other Senators. There won't be many of them, so the choice will not be difficult. He'll be a great help in voting. You'll vote as he does for the first few weeks of the session, until you get other sources of help.

Soon after your arrival in the capital, stop in to see the Auditor.

"Hello, Senator. Just dropped in to say hello."

Don't refer to yourself as Senator; that was his job, and at the beginning of the session he will be attacked by melancholy whenever he is reminded that it is no longer his. Your demeanor also lets him know you realize you can never fill his shoes. Let him tell you about how difficult his job is. Sympathize with his problems. You'll stop in from time to time as the session progresses, and he'll tell you the same thing. Might as well get used to it early.

The Senate chamber itself is decorated in what might be called "Turn of the Century Patriotic." There are pictures, flags, and the like, designed to enhance the basic image. There may even be eagles carved in the plaster of the ceiling and a mural depicting the most recent Indian massacre.

Some legislature, at one time or another, spent a lot of the State's money to make the chamber dignified. They were also practical, however, and installed dark red carpeting to help conceal some of the larger blood stains. The desks have been modernized only to the extent that a microphone is installed at each of them. Each desk is large enough to accommodate the stacks of printed copies of bills that will accumulate during the session as well as your last bowling trophy and perhaps a banana given you by a grateful constituent.

There will usually be a lot of activity during the sessions, activity other than that being directed by the President. Gallery visitors may think it unseemly for a Senator to leave his seat to talk to someone when a bill is being read. Actually, the Senator knows the contents of the bill. The reading is a formality that must be observed because it is in the Constitution.

As we have indicated, the more important Senate business takes place outside the Senate chamber. The room itself, however, is handy for making speeches when groups of your constituents are in the gallery, for honoring visiting dignitaries, and for voting.

Only members of the Senate are allowed access to the floor while it is in session. Before it convenes each day there will be a bustle of visitors to the floor—such as lobbyists exacting their price for last night's dinner, party leaders exacting their price for help during the last election, or a page bringing help to recover from last night's revelry.

Former members of the body are sometimes accorded the courtesy of access to the floor during the sessions. This makes them particularly valuable as lobbyists. Then they do not have to arrange elaborate sets of signals to communicate with key people from the gallery.

Other lobbyists will sit in the gallery when a matter of particular moment to them is being discussed. You can tell how it is going for them by the varieties of coloring their faces take on. Also in the gallery may be members of groups that support certain legislation. For example, a bill dealing with minimum salaries for police forces will guarantee a large attendance of the constabulary in full regalia. They will respond to favorable or unfavorable comment on the matter at hand much as they would respond at a baseball game. This adds to the charm of the chamber.

You will be much aware of the gallery in the beginning, but you will begin to get used to the visitors as time goes on. And by the end of the session the Bill Book on your desk will have grown sufficiently large to provide you with a secure hiding place. You can always stand up to be seen, if you are tall enough.

When you arrive for the opening session, you may be tempted to display the elaborate Certificate of Election you received, thinking it a means of gaining entrance to the chamber. Don't. The Sergeant-at-Arms will not require it, and he'll

"Pressure groups attempt to mold public opinion to accomplish their own aims, and at any given moment it seems that government is the result of a compromise between conflicting pressure groups." — Temporary National Economic Committee, Seventy-Sixth Congress

think you're some kind of nut. He's an important individual. Not only does he open the door to members and keep it closed to nonmembers, he also brings important messages from people outside who want to see you or talk with you on the phone. These people probably won't want to talk about the matter being treated on the floor, but you must always respond. Even if it's only your wife telling you to bring home a loaf of bread.

The first few weeks of the session will be the most difficult, especially when you are required to vote on bills. A few rules will guide you through safely.

RULE 14. *Never explain your vote at the session.*

You will have a tendency to be most sincere at the time a bill is being debated. You can think of much better reasons for your vote after the session has ended. It's a temptation to use that microphone so conveniently placed in front of you. Keep it furled, especially at the beginning.

RULE 15. *Never cast the deciding vote.*

If you do, you can be sure your name will be in the papers, but you can never be sure what they'll say. If necessary, arrange to be in the cloakroom until the issue has been decided. You can record your vote later, when no one really cares about it.

RULE 16. *Rely on expert opinion.*

There are a number of people whose only purpose is to help you reach the right decisions on legislation. They represent certain specific interests that want bills passed for their own purposes. They really have the good of the entire state at heart. Well, at least, their particular portion of it. Besides, if you're not nice to the lobbyists, they may cut off those free dinners.

Your Political Wheel will be helpful, too. As we have said, he will make certain suggestions from time to time. These times will most often be during voting. If there is a conflict between the Wheel and the lobbyists, you will have to arrange a case of twenty-four-hour beri-beri. Conflicts won't occur often. These men are all public-spirited citizens; they are all after the same things.

For those few instances when you have to rely on your personal knowledge to vote on a bill, there are some guidelines. It is always safe to vote for expanded services. However, never vote in favor of the appropriations necessary to put the new services into effect. People understand things done for them; they don't understand paying for them. Of course, vote Yea on bills dealing with adoption of the "Pledge of Allegiance," improved maternity care, or solar exposure for the underprivileged. Al-

77

ways vote Nay on bills involving taxes and all those you don't understand. Of course, most will fall into this last category.

Be patient. During the first session of your term you'll gather knowledge you'll need to become a Senate Hero in your second session, right before you have to run for re-election. You'll also learn about the men who share with you the responsibility of Senator.

Use your notebook wisely.

10

⊠ And then there's the press

You have to have an image. We don't mean a statue in the park. A public image. Another self. A phantom that is you to the voters. It must be good and positive and appealing. In short, you must

RULE 17. *Develop the right image.*

There is no real secret about the kind of image you need. The mold was begun by George Washington, filled in by Andrew Jackson and Abraham Lincoln, and brought up to date by Dwight D. Eisenhower. You must appear to be trustworthy, loyal, helpful, friendly, courteous, kind, obedient, cheerful, thrifty, brave, clean and reverent. You're panicking now. We didn't say you had to have all those qualities, just so long as you seem to have them.

You develop your image not through the voters, but through the newspapers. Now, the newspaper men know you're not all these things. No one is. So don't try to fool them. Make no mistake. There is only one way to develop the right image. The press. Newspapers.

You know, of course, that newspapers actually devote much of their hard news to politics and government. But you are just a freshman Senator. So if you make the papers at all, it will probably be in a squib buried among the crossword puzzles, comic strips and recipes. That's O.K. For now. At this point, you need only to

RULE 18. *Cultivate the press.*

Political reporters and editors have one of the most difficult of jobs; they have to listen to politicians. Then, when they finally hear something important, or interesting, or even startling, they have to go to the trouble of translating it into those terse semi-sentences that pass for prose in newspapers. If you manage to understand reporters and editors, they will be inclined to help you.

You can begin to cultivate them in the Capitol pressroom. This is a room much like any other—

"The effect of a newspaper is not only to suggest the same purpose to a great number of persons, but to furnish means for executing in common the designs which they may have singly conceived."—*Democracy In America* by Alexis de Tocqueville

ceilings, walls, a floor, maybe a door. Desks are cluttered with newspapers, each reporter trying to find out what all the others said yesterday. There is a background whine, created by the loud-speakers that carry the debates from the two chambers. If something important happens, the reporters will jump up and dash to the appropriate place. Normally, however, they sit in the press-room waiting for news, inspiration, or lunch. A few will be tussling with typewriters—preparing a story, a column or a laundry list.

The dedication of the press is such that the reporters don't leave the pressroom during the hours the legislature is in session. So they cannot escape to eat. You can help them a little by arranging with a local caterer to provide sustenance through the dreary hours. Alcohol is reputed to be a good source of quick energy.

You can feel free to join them. In fact an occasional repetition will give you *carte blanche* in the pressroom, which will enable you to avoid exposure to school children in the gallery who sit and watch you nibbling your lunch.

You've already learned the basic rules for cultivating people; now apply them in the capital. Get to know the reporters and editors, especially those who work for important papers in your city. Important papers are those of large circulation that tend to follow the general line laid down by your party. Some papers are thoroughly committed to one party or another. But cultivating the reporters who can never actively support you is still of value. You may be able to insure that they will not work actively against you.

Along with the basic methods of cultivation there are one or two that work particularly well with reporters.

RULE 19. *Be accessible.*

Oh, you'll see them often enough, in the pressroom or in bars, but we mean that you should talk freely with them. Of course, you never say anything that you don't want to see in the next morning's paper, but there are secrets and inside information that you can "leak" every now and then.

The important thing about secrets is to let reporters find out about them from you first. This is not snitching. (That's something else altogether.) This is merely making it just a little easier for them to do their job. They'll repay you with an occasional mention in their news stories or columns. It won't be much, but it will be a start. Anyway, the habit will be forming. If they start saying nice things about you, they can never stop.

When you get to know each reporter, you begin to learn those causes in which he is particularly interested. A little homework from time to time should make it possible for you to speak profoundly on the areas of each man's interest. They will begin to respect you . . . and think you know as much about everything. This will mark you as a comer, and they'll say so.

Later, you will want editorials in your favor. Don't make the mistake of trying to plant editorials, unless your uncle owns the paper. One legislator planted a piece of information that led to editorials in all four of his city's papers. They appeared on the same day. He planned it that way. His retirement soon followed.

Editorials will come later when you are doing things that will arouse sufficient interest. We'll show you how. In the meantime just be happy to get to know the press and be satisfied with a brief mention of yourself once in a while. You musn't move too fast.

11

⊠ Becoming a senate hero

You learned in the first session who makes things happen in the Senate. In your second session you will make them happen. You must become a Senate Hero before you can become Governor. To do so, you need three groups backing you: the press, your colleagues, and the legislative advisors.

In the last session you cultivated the press and impressed them a bit with your voting record. Now you must

RULE 20. *Activate the press in your behalf.*

To do this you need only (a) catch a bad bill and

(b) sponsor a good one. These two maneuvers are best done in committee. As you know, a committee is supposed to discuss the merits of legislation and make recommendations to the full Senate. It doesn't really work that way. Most bills merely pause momentarily in committee and are passed, good or bad, on the assumption that the Governor will veto the bad ones. No point in offending your colleagues who sponsor the bills. You can always claim that the Governor doesn't have good legislative rapport.

There will be many bad bills from which to select one you can safely oppose. As a member of the Senate Committee on Public Health, Aid and Safety, you will easily find a bill, say one dealing with safety devices on home garbage disposal units, that makes a mistake—inadvertently changes the size of the standard sink drain, for example. In the committee hearing you rise.

"Mr. Chairman, this is a dangerous bill. If it passes, the sanctity of every home in the state will be threatened. It is our sworn duty to protect each and every citizen. We must defeat this bill now. We cannot allow special interests to impede the will of the majority and hamper progress in our great state."

The next morning the papers will say,

SMALL DEFEATS DRAIN BILL
Senator Franklin Pierce Small today fought

"...I can see what the law is like.... There ain't ever enough ... to cover the case...."—*All the King's Men* by Robert Penn Warren

valiantly and finally defeated the Kitchen Drain Bill that would affect every home and cost thousands of unnecessary dollars. The Senator said, "It's dangerous . . . every home is threatened."

Excellent. Now to get a good bill through. You must select one that has universal appeal but will cost little to implement. Let's say a bill to regulate sanitary conditions in diaper service establishments. In committee you announce,

"This bill will protect mothers and children from the scourge of infectious diseases."

If another member, sensing a chance for some publicity, complains that there's too much government regulation already, you respond,

"Does the distinguished Senator from Chillicothe suggest he is against protecting mothers and helpless infants from death or worse?"

The next day the papers will say,

SMALL PROTECTS MOTHERS

Franklin Pierce Small, fast becoming one of the most influential Senators, today pushed through a bill to establish adequate sanitary conditions in diaper services. He was opposed by the Senator from Chillicothe, who is known to have close connections with the diaper interests.

See, we told you it would be worthwhile to cultivate the press, even though you didn't get much ink at first. Now you'll be in news stories, reporters' columns and even editorials. You have the press in your camp.

Having activated the press, you can begin to concentrate on your fellow Senators. Go to your close friend, the Auditor.

"Senator,"
—he still likes that title best—
"you've been thinking about bringing the state parks under your office, haven't you?"

He hasn't. He wasn't thinking about being Auditor either until you suggested it. But he wants to expand the influence of his office, especially if it means more patronage under his control.

You had already hired a firm of management consultants to justify placing a control of the state parks in the Auditor's office. Management consultants will justify anything you want them to. So give their report to the Auditor and offer to sponsor the bill incorporating its suggestions.

You'll have no trouble getting the bill passed. Your colleagues will be interested in fiscal improvement, especially if it means more patronage jobs. The Auditor will reward your patriotism by making you the dispenser of the new jobs in the Senate. If the Governor objects, a few remarks about his highway bill should bring him around.

While developing your relations with the press and your colleagues, you are also maintaining good relations with the Third House. Lobbyists are the most influential group in the capital. They cannot, however, introduce legislation in their own names. Senators are expected to take any heat from the press. You can be helpful to the lobbyists by making yourself available as a sponsor for their bills.

Don't worry about the content of the bills. They will see to that. They won't submit any bad legislation; they, too, are patriots.

By the end of the second session, you will be a Senate Hero, applauded by the press, respected by your colleagues, and backed by the lobbyists. All you need do now is be re-elected Senator. Then you will be but two steps away from Governor.

12

⊠ Winning re-election

Between legislative sessions, spend your time maintaining connections with the Ward Bosses in your district, and developing new connections with helpful citizens, especially those who have contributed to your campaigns. You've reached the point where you're allowed to enter that PRIVATE room at ward headquarters. Those two young men in the corner are now busily arguing about whether you follow the political philosophy of Plato or Locke. Continue to avoid them.

You have no trouble being nominated by your party for re-election to the Senate. Even those who don't know the rules know they can't beat you. But the Other Party may try to unseat you to regain their lost majority. You will therefore have to conduct a general election campaign.

Essentially, the general election campaign will be different from the primary campaign only in that you now take your appeal directly to the voters. You will, of course, prepare a brochure and other materials that point with pride to your distinguished record. The newspapers will continue to applaud you, which will be most helpful. In any event, you still live in a safe district.

Your exposure to the voting public will be concentrated into those few weeks that are an election campaign. Between elections the public doesn't care what you do. So it's important that you create an outstanding impression during campaigns.

RULE 21. *Run on your record.*

At public meetings the best vote-getting tool you have is your record as a Senator. That's why we went to so much trouble to make a record for you. Most of those who attend the meetings will be your supporters anyway, and for them you need only smile and wave to earn vast and thunderous applause.

To get a meeting really rolling, arrange to have someone ask a spontaneous question after you have completed the speech discussed in Appendix II.

"Senator Small, we know how valiantly you

"We are the Sheep, the Cow, and the Hog . . . it is we three who are blended in man's being. . . ." Then the Sheep said: "I am the conscience of Mankind. My desire is for quietness. . . ." The Cow said: "I am the mind of mankind; I desire quietness. I dislike that which is unfamiliar. . . ." And the Hog said: "I am the body of mankind . . . the less said about me the better . . . I prefer quietness . . . as only thrives in deep mire. . . ."—*Smire   An Acceptance in the Third Person* by James Branch Cabell

fought to stop the insidious Kitchen Drain Bill, even though it might have jeopardized your entire political career. We're proud of a man who will not submit to the threats of vicious hoodlums who only want an opportunity to prey on the public. We know your distinguished war record and your history of business success. But, tell us, Senator, aren't you making many personal sacrifices to serve in public office?"

After the vast applause subsides, you reply,

"You're a public-spirited citizen, sir. And you're absolutely right. But no sacrifice is too great."

You certainly don't have to be indirect about a question like that.

At some point, probably as the thunderous applause quiets, a heckler will arise,

"Senator, in your last campaign you said you were against the encroaching powers of the government, and you were out to stop it from meddling in private business. Yet you sponsored a bill regulating diaper services. How do you explain this?"

To show you're not afraid of the question, hold up your hand to quiet the crowd, just before they lynch the questioner.

"I'm not afraid to answer the poor man's question. I think that government ought to do only what the people can't do for themselves, and private enterprise should be allowed to flourish. Yet our mothers and children must be protected from candidates that existed in the Middle Ages."

Ah! You're ahead of us, you've learned.

RULE 22. *Always use the balanced sentence.*

You know, of course, that a balanced sentence is one that neatly straddles both sides of a question and can be used backwards or forwards, as required. For example, in the answer to that last question, if your audience is a PTA group, you will say,

"It's the just duty of the government of this state to protect our mothers and children from conditions that existed in the Middle Ages. Yet private enterprises must be allowed to flourish and the government should do only what the people can't do for themselves."

Chances are that some well-meaning citizen will ask what he thinks is an honest question:

"Senator, you sponsored a bill putting control of the state parks in the Auditor's office. Couldn't they be run more economically by the Conservation Department?"

95

There will be no applause here.

"I'm glad to hear from a thoughtful voter. The state parks are the property of the people and should be open to them at any time, consistent with maximum safety and reasonable operating expenses."

Good work. Not only have you mastered the balanced sentence, but you've applied to it the indirect answer.

You're making remarkable progress. You're ready now to return to the Capitol as the leader of the Senate and ... but we're jumping a little ahead.

13

⊠ Onward and upward

As a returning Senator you have a right to feel proudly conscious of your position. Junior members will be watching you to see how they should vote. In fact, you are now at the height of your power. If you stay in the Senate too long, your colleagues will get to know you too well, and your prestige will suffer. Now is the time to move. Become President Pro Tem of the Senate.

You've already laid a good foundation on which to build your attempt at the President's chair. But you must now raise the rest of the structure. You go back to the three groups you need, the press, your colleagues, and the lobbyists, to insure that you will be the choice of each of them.

Before you make your move, provide yourself

with the basic lever you'll need.

RULE 23. *Have a noble reason.*

Your reason does not necessarily have to be believed by everyone, so long as it is believable. You want to be President of the Senate because you feel that you might make a contribution, for example. Or because you feel that the Senate needs the kind of leadership you can give. Or because prominent people all over the state have suggested it. Reasonable ambition is understandable as long as its stated end is the common good.

Your first step is to use the press, culminating the process started with cultivation and solidified by activation. You cultivated them in your first term, and you activated them when you became a Senate Hero. Of course, you'll use a paper that has supported you actively, one that shares your political persuasion. You'll also be sure that it is a paper with influence over the party all over the state.

See the editor or publisher, whoever makes general policy for the paper. Tell him you want to discuss the coming legislative session.

After a while, you will say,

"I'm thinking I might be able to do more good as President Pro Tem. What do you think?"

He may not answer at that time. He may, instead, launch into a discourse about possible legislation for or against some of his favorite crusades. Don't worry. A few days later his paper will carry an editorial suggesting you as an outstanding choice for President Pro Tem.

Before the papers announce your candidacy, contact the other leaders of the Senate from your party. Understand, you don't need all the votes; the majority party elects a President. Only one more than half of your party's Senators can control the caucus.

Of course, these Senate leaders will be the ones who will have received the most jobs in the Auditor's State Parks Department. When you call them:

"George, do you still have those eight fellows working down at River Fork?"

If he says yes—

"Good. Just wanted to check. By the way, I want you to be one of the first to know I'm going for President. Hope I'll have your support."

You will. He wants to keep those eight jobs. But if he says he doesn't have all eight jobs—

"What! The Auditor promised me. It must be some mistake. Tell you what. I think there are three additional jobs down there. I'll get the ones you lost back and the other three

99

" . . . party organization consists of dispersed and loosely linked centers of power. . . . Nice calculations of strength and status must be made in the allocation of patronage among claimants for recognition, and precautions must be taken to assure clearance with those whose status in the party suffices to command that they be consulted about appointments."—*Politics, Parties and Pressure Groups* by V. O. Key, Jr.

besides."

Do it. Then call back and get his support. If
you have trouble with the Auditor, tell him the
State Treasurer is becoming interested in state
parks.

Now for the most important group. Lobbyists do
not elect Presidents of the Senate, but one cannot
be elected without their support. Call or see each
one.

"Dan, I've been troubled about the way
Hogan [the previous President] handled your
bill last time. Been thinking I might be able to
do a better job for you."

No lobbyist likes the way his bill was handled,
whether it passed or not. There was an amendment tacked on, or something was changed, or
the Governor vetoed it. Don't worry about your
ambition showing, he understands.

Once elected President Pro Tem of the Senate,
you could be only one step away from the Governorship. It depends. Chances are that your state
will have already done away with the office of
Lieutenant Governor. If not, it will be on the verge
of doing so; and as President Pro Tem, you can
help things along.

Lieutenant Governor is one of those decorative
offices that was developed because it seemed like
a good idea at the time. Over the years his real

functions have diminished to the point where they could be carried out by a bright Eagle Scout. In some states they were. It's an office with little political future and no governmental present.

Some states have relegated the Lieutenant Governorship to nothing more than a waiting job. Waiting for the Governor to leave his office vacant, of course. So it is reasonable to ask why he should succeed to the Governorship, compared to such an important individual as President Pro Tem of the Senate? You agree?

It might have taken a constitutional amendment in your state, but it might only have been one small change in the statutes. In any case, what's important is that the President Pro Tem of the Senate be first in the line of succession to the Governorship. If he's not, you'll have the additional problem of making the necessary changes. This will mean only a slight delay while the amendment is ratified. In the meantime, you are the President Pro Tem, which means you're running the Senate.

Of course, you have responsibilities as President, but you won't be in the position too long, so they needn't worry you. We will pass on a few pointers so that you won't be embarrassed.

RULE 24. *Use Murphy's rules of order (revised).*

Murphy is your sister's first husband, and he

doesn't know anything about parliamentary procedure. Therefore his rules are invaluable. Make the revisions as you go along. As President, you will have to make decisions about calling bills, recognizing members, and the like. Decide any way you want, and refer to Murphy's rules as your authority. Anybody who mentions that Murphy's rules are not in the Senate library won't be invited to your suite for hors d'oeuvres anymore. It is wise to bone up particularly on motions to adjourn and questioning a quorum. They can get you off the hook on many a hot bill.

As President of the Senate, you'll be summoned often to the Governor's office. You will have dinner in the mansion. Your wife and his wife will become friendly. These are absolutely necessary for the next step. You've done well, and you're very nearly there. But the road now becomes precipitous. Be very, very careful.

14

⊠ Governor!

Begin the final step in your quest for success by becoming familiar with Freud. All that's really required is a smattering of knowledge on ego and the sex drive. You can obtain an inexpensive paperback copy of Freud's works. While you're at the bookstore you might buy several more copies of *Politics from the Inside Up*. It's really the least you can do to repay us.

The sex drive and the ego are separate in most persons. When the two come together, a love of self results. This unification has taken place in most politicians. The Governor is one of the rare exceptions. So are you. That's why he is, and you will be, Governor.

As chief executive, the Governor spends his days

at the Capitol and his nights making civic and political speeches. You can cultivate the Governor's wife while he's gone.

RULE 25. *Don't give in to temptation.*

The Governor's wife is not a Tinker Toy. And you want to be Governor, not one of the great lovers of history.

Your purpose is to implant a desire in the Governor's wife. A desire for her husband not to be Governor. Take her for a walk on a moonless night. You venture,

"Moonlight on the Potomac is beautiful this time of the year."

She'll sigh, wistfully, as the novelists say.

Approach her when she is left all alone at a cocktail party attended by Party members:

"At Washington cocktail parties, over half the guests are from other countries. It's very exciting."

She'll answer,

"Nothing but stupid ward heelers here. Everyone looking for a job."

Keep this up for several months. By the time you're ready to make a move, she'll have already packed her bags.

105

You'll know when the time has arrived: the Governor summons you to his office. Usually he invites you.

"Dammit, Small. What are you trying to pull here? There's no place for me in Washington. Not yet anyway. The way you've been brainwashing my wife she wants me to move there and go to work."

Cast out the bait.

"But Governor, I'd be the last to suggest you leave the State, unless it was a move up. You're ready for the national scene."

He agrees.

"You're right. And I'd certainly like to go to Washington. Wife and I could be together much more there. But I can see through you. Since that last constitutional Amendment you're the next in line for Governor if I resign."

He's hooked. Play him carefully.

"I've thought of becoming Governor. But of course only because I had bigger things in mind for you. By the way, have you signed the bill giving a new Chief Justice of the State Supreme Court life tenure and doubling the salary?"

He'll protest.

106

"Sign it? It's out of the question. Against anything I ever stood for. What's that got to do with it anyway?"

Haul him in.

"Well, if that bill became law, I understand Senator Byron would like to retire, get away from Washington, and spend the rest of his life on the bench."

Wheels will begin turning. He smells a deal, and at this level, deals become rather complex. Now he sees it! He wants to be Senator, you want to be Governor. A U.S. Senator wants to become Chief Justice of the State. The Governor need only sign the bill that doubles the Chief Justice's salary and give him life tenure, and there will be a vacancy in the U.S. Senate.

When he resigns as Governor, you would take his place. And you'd appoint someone to fill the Senate vacancy. Who'd be more qualified to be a Senator than an ex-Governor?

So it happens.

First the bill is signed. Then the Senator resigns. The Senator is appointed Chief Justice. The Governor resigns. You move up to fill the vacancy. You appoint a new U.S. Senator. The ex-Governor.

As your chauffeur drives the big, black Cadillac (no longer an incidental expense) over the highways of what is now *your* state, take a moment to reflect a bit. Is this not a land of opportunity?

" . . . individuals having any advantage . . . have the best chance of surviving. . . . This preservation of favorable individual differences and variations, and the destruction of those which are injurious, I have called Natural Selection, or the Survival of the Fittest."—*The Origin of the Species* by Charles Darwin

Where else can wenches become fair ladies, mail boys corporate executives, and Assistant Precinct Captains Governors of great states—with nothing but ability, pluck, and determination?

15

⊠ After Governor?

You're on your own. We'll take you no further.
Our conscience is bothering us already.

⊠ Appendix 1

Your short speech

Always make this short speech to gatherings attended by party workers. This will probably be the most attentive group to whom you'll be able to speak. Don't make the mistake of taking advantage of them. You cannot possibly say anything they haven't heard many times before. You can't even phrase things in a way that will be new to them. They have heard all the speeches and oratorical pyrotechnics there are.

You will do far better to keep your speech short as long as it contains all the expected elements. We advise memorizing the speech now; it will serve you well for many years. Pay particular attention to the footnotes.

"I'm real happy[1] to be here in the ——[2] ward and spend a few minutes with all of you, especially my good friend ——,[3] who heads up this fine[4] organization.

"In fact, if it weren't for ——[5] and you loyal party members who work with him, our party wouldn't be in the great position it is today. You know I wouldn't lie to you. We're in great shape *this* time.[6] This time we're going to win, and we're going to win big.[7] If you give your utmost, as we who are candidates are doing, we'll elect our ticket from top to bottom.[8]

"I've been around the district, and I know what's happening. The voters are ready for our party.[9]

[1]Everybody will start this way, but don't try to vary it, it serves as a warning signal to your audience.

[2]Always, always mention the ward number, and never, never make a mistake. You can write the proper number on the palm of your hand, if necessary. Use washable ink.

[3]This is the Ward Boss. Use his full name here.

[4]Add as many other adjectives as you care to. However, after a string of eight or so, they begin to lose their effect.

[5]Ward Boss, again. But use only his first name; it shows you're good friends.

[6]Wait for the applause to stop.

[7]Wait for the applause to stop.

[8]Wait for the applause to stop.

[9]You understand that this speech can be used for either party.

112

They're fed up with the graft and corruption the Other Party is giving them in place of good government. They don't want any more of it. So when you're out there wearing out your shoe leather, they'll listen to what you have to say.[10]

"It's hard work.[11] I know that, and you know I know it, but the cause is just. We're fighting the good fight.[12]

"———[13] says you're going to carry big for me here in the ———[14] ward. And I know you are. I can feel it in the air of this room. I can smell a victory,[15] not only for me[16] as State Senator, but for all the fine candidates on this platform with me now,[17] and every candidate our party wants to see nominated.

"And you know I won't forget you either. Never.

[10]Start the paragraph talking softly; gradually add volume so that by this point you're at a near shout.

[11]Put extra emphasis on "hard."

[12]You can here refer to the government scandal, in the Other Party, of course, currently in the headlines. This is optional.

[13]Ward Boss again. If he has a nickname, use it here; if not, add an appropriate string of adjectives.

[14]Check the palm of your hand. Be sure.

[15]It is not desirable here to mention the real atmosphere of the room.

[16]In your first campaign, mention your name here. After the first, it's optional.

[17]Bow, right and left.

———[18] knows that if he ever wants anything from me, all he has to do is ask. In fact, I'll be available to all of you, any time. My phone number will be the same after the election as it is now.[19]

"Well, I know that the mind can't absorb more than the seat[20] can endure, and those chairs get pretty hard. There are other fine candidates here who have something to say to you, and I won't use up their time. But keep up the good work, and as ———[21] knows, you won't be forgotten when the jobs, favors and other just rewards are passed out."[22]

[18]Ward Boss. First name.

[19]Don't bother to mention that your number is unlisted.

[20]Seat. There may be ladies present.

[21]Ward Boss. Full name.

[22]Shake hands with the Ward Boss and as many other people as you can reach.

☒ Appendix 2

Notes on Long Speeches

Long speeches are usually made to general audiences at dinners. The dinner, in politics, has replaced the rally and torchlight parade of days gone by. High prices cannot be charged to attend a rally. As a result, most dinners will be attended by party members. The audience is therefore different from one composed of party workers. The distinction is, of course, subtle. Party members may be workers, but they may also be leaders, contributors, or just plain citizens. Very few who attend dinners are workers or citizens.

The general audience expects you to do more than prove that you can speak American. They expect to be entertained, excited a little, and told how wonderful *they* are. Doing all this does tend to necessitate a speech longer than the one you make to the party workers.

You'll see that we cannot write this speech for you. There are too many differences in audiences in different places, in orators, and even in the subject matter to be covered. We have provided a handy-dandy checklist that you or your speech writer can use in writing or delivering an address. If you do not write your speeches yourself, be sure you read them at least once before you deliver them. Many a candidate has been sabotaged by a speech writer who was unhappy, unknowledgable, or showing off his Ph.D.

You should practice delivering your speech, especially at the beginning of your career. It's important that you develop just the right tone, voice quality, and facial expressions. Political speeches are not really delivered, at that. They are played, like short dramas with a single actor—you. As you gain experience, you'll find that certain phrases, expressions, and arias are best for you. Note them carefully so that by the time you have run in two or three campaigns you can piece the best parts together into a single speech. You will then be equipped for speech making for the rest of your career.

This checklist will help you over the initial hurdles.

SPEECH DELIVERY CHECKLIST

___ Never make a political speech without a lectern. A lectern is a place on which the speech rests as you read it, and on which you can rest when you're delivering your fifth speech of the night.

___ Always use a microphone. A short financial discussion with the engineer who operates the sound system can add much tone, volume, and resonance to your voice.

___ Look at your audience while you're speaking. This gives you an essential personal contact and keeps people from trying to sneak out.

___ If you're tempted to use gestures, have a movie made of yourself speaking. This will probably dissuade you.

___ A few dollars invested in acting lessons will do much to improve your speeches.

___ Vary the volume and tone often. You're not there to drone a lullaby.

___ Use well-timed pauses to win applause. You'll be judged by the number of times your speech is interrupted. It's not undesirable to insure spontaneous applause.

___ Keep your hands the hell out of the way.

___ Don't rustle papers in the mike. Sometimes these noises are mistaken by sensitive people for parts of your speech. You don't want to be misquoted.

___ Invest whatever is necessary on good dental work.

___ At the end of your speech, have your spontaneous applauders provide you with a standing ovation.

— Remember the microphone will still be alive after you have finished speaking. Save value judgments for backstage.

SPEECH WRITING CHECKLIST

— Acknowledge everybody at the speakers' table. The one you miss will miss you.

— Always start with a joke, or course, but make it right. It has to get a laugh; therefore we suggest it be funny. Test a joke several times with smaller groups before using it in a major address.

— If away from your own city, say a few nice things about the town you're in. A brief look at a local history book or the statue in the town square will supply ample clues.

— Build your speech around a current happening that is or can be made to appear gravely important. This will get attention and enable you to use your full range of emotions.

— Use a matter the press is unanimous about, not something supported only by the Chillicothe *Weekly*, unless you're in Chillicothe.

— Write in at least one subject about which you can become justifiably angry.

— Write a part that makes you a little humble. A little—don't overdo it.

— Use as many balanced sentences as time will

permit.

— Break up the serious parts of the speech with a joke in the middle. Again, it must be funny.

— Don't use the same joke twice in the same speech, however, no matter how good a response you got.

— Build to an emotional climax. Noble words and allusions will help you to achieve the right feeling. Cry, if you can.

⊠ Acknowledgements

Although it is impossible to thank personally all those who have helped in the preparation of this book, some deserve special mention. Mr. Lynn Williams made many useful and usable suggestions. Professor Walter Johnson, Mr. Robert Cronson, Professor John Hope Franklin, and Mrs. A. V. Dilzer were kind enough to read and comment on parts of the manuscript. Mrs. Toni Kaufman performed well beyond the call of duty in typing the manuscript. The staff of Follett Publishing Company was most helpful.

We cannot say enough about the part played by our wives, Lucy Reum and Nancy Mattran, in the making of this book. They gave us the encouragement that only wives can give. This book is as much theirs as it is ours.

We also wish to thank the following for their kind permission to quote from copyrighted material:

The Free Press, publishers of *Politics*: *Who Gets What, When, How*, by Harold D. Lasswell. Copyright © 1951 by The Free Press, Inc.

The University of Chicago Press, publishers

We wish to thank all these people and the many others whose interest, enthusiasm for the project, and confidence in us played such an important part in the completion of the work.